Major European
Union Nations

# MAJOR
# EUROPEAN UNION
# NATIONS

Austria
Belgium
Czech Republic
Denmark
France
Germany
Greece
Ireland

Italy
The Netherlands
Poland
Portugal
Spain
Sweden
United Kingdom

# FRANCE

by
Jeanine Sanna and Shaina C. Indovino

Mason Crest

Major European Union Nations

Mason Crest
370 Reed Road, Broomall,
Pennsylvania 19008
www.masoncrest.com

Printed in the Hashemite Kingdom of Jordan.

First printing
9 8 7 6 5 4 3 2 1

Library of Congress Cataloging-in-Publication Data

Sanna, Jeanine.
France / by Jeanine Sanna and Shaina C. Indovino.
   p. cm. —  (The European Union: political, social, and economic cooperation)
Includes index.
ISBN 978-1-4222-2242-3 (hardcover) — ISBN 978-1-4222-2231-7 (series hardcover) — ISBN 978-1-4222-9266-2 (ebook)
1. France—Juvenile literature.  I. Indovino, Shaina Carmel. II. Title.
DC17.S282 2012
944—dc22

2010051290

Produced by Harding House Publishing Services, Inc.
www.hardinghousepages.com
Interior layout by Micaela Sanna.
Cover design by Torque Advertising + Design.

# CONTENTS

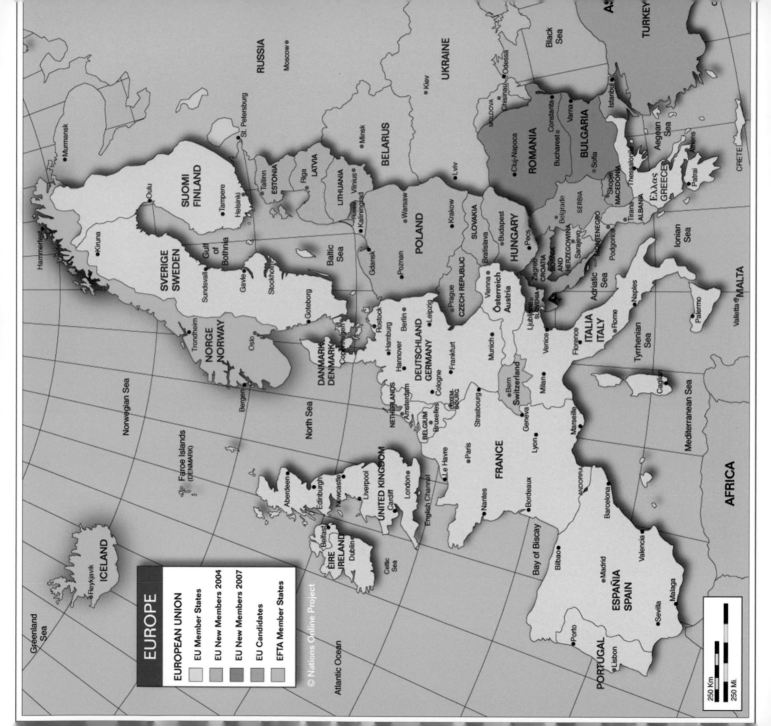

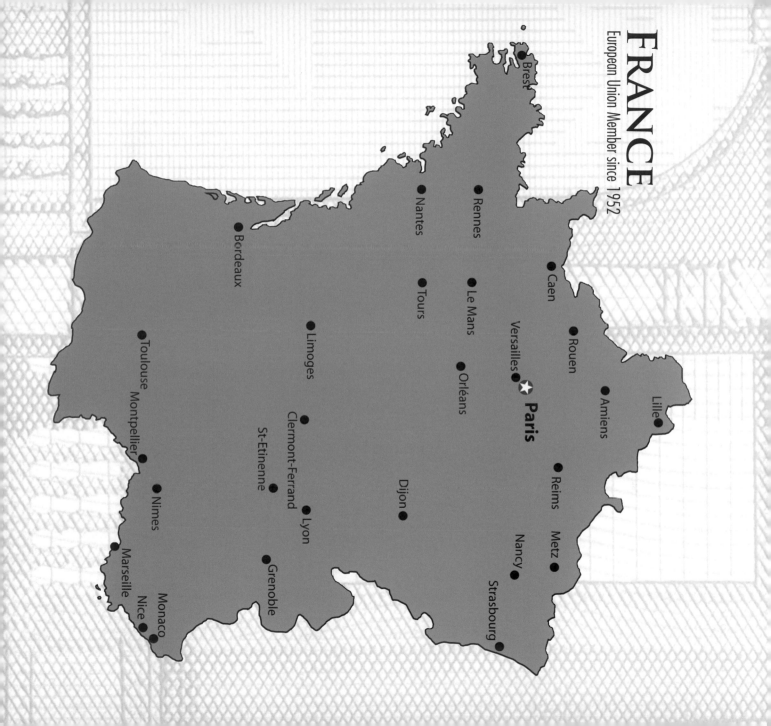

# INTRODUCTION

Sixty years ago, Europe lay scarred from the battles of the Second World War. During the next several years, a plan began to take shape that would unite the countries of the European continent so that future wars would be inconceivable. On May 9, 1950, French Foreign Minister Robert Schuman issued a declaration calling on France, Germany, and other European countries to pool together their coal and steel production as "the first concrete foundation of a European federation." "Europe Day" is celebrated each year on May 9 to commemorate the beginning of the European Union (EU).

The EU consists of twenty-seven countries, spanning the continent from Ireland in the west to the border of Russia in the east. Eight of the ten most recently admitted EU member states are former communist regimes that were behind the Iron Curtain for most of the latter half of the twentieth century.

Any European country with a democratic government, a functioning market economy, respect for fundamental rights, and a government capable of implementing EU laws and policies may apply for membership. Bulgaria and Romania joined the EU in 2007. Croatia, Serbia, Turkey, Iceland, Montenegro, and Macedonia have also embarked on the road to EU membership.

While the EU began as an idea to ensure peace in Europe through interconnected economies, it has evolved into so much more today:

- Citizens can travel freely throughout most of the EU without carrying a passport and without stopping for border checks.

- EU citizens can live, work, study, and retire in another EU country if they wish.

- The euro, the single currency accepted throughout seventeen of the EU countries (with more to come), is one of the EU's most tangible achievements, facilitating commerce and making possible a single financial market that benefits both individuals and businesses.

- The EU ensures cooperation in the fight against cross-border crime and terrorism.

- The EU is spearheading world efforts to preserve the environment.

- As the world's largest trading bloc, the EU uses its influence to promote fair rules for world trade, ensuring that globalization also benefits the poorest countries.

- The EU is already the world's largest donor of humanitarian aid and development assistance, providing around 60 percent of global official development assistance to developing countries in 2011.

The EU is not a nation intended to replace existing nations. The EU is unique—its member countries have established common institutions to which they delegate some of their sovereignty so that decisions on matters of joint interest can be made democratically at the European level.

Europe is a continent with many different traditions and languages, but with shared values such as democracy, freedom, and social justice, cherished values well known to North Americans. Indeed, the EU motto is "United in Diversity."

Enjoy your reading. Take advantage of this chance to learn more about Europe and the EU!

Ambassador John Bruton,
Former EU President and Prime Minister of Ireland

Paris, France.

# MODERN ISSUES

Jean-Pierre has a lot of questions, but his parents are finding it hard to give him clear answers. Recently, many families who live near his communities were forced to leave with very short notice. Jean-Pierre saw kids his age from these families every day—but then one day, they were all gone.

# THE FORMATION OF THE EUROPEAN UNION

The EU is a confederation of European nations that continues to grow. All countries that enter the EU agree to follow common laws about foreign security policies. They also agree to cooperate on legal matters that go on within the EU. The European Council meets to discuss all international matters and make decisions about them. Each country's own concerns and interests are important, though. And apart from legal and financial issues, the EU tries to uphold values such as peace and solidarity, human dignity, freedom, and equality. All member countries remain autonomous. This means that they generally keep their own laws and regulations. The EU becomes involved only if there is an international issue or if a member country has violated the principles of the union.

The idea for a union among European nations was first mentioned after World War II. The war had devastated much of Europe, both physically and financially. In 1950, French foreign minister Robert Schuman suggested that France and West Germany combine their coal and steel industries under one authority. Both countries would have control over the industries. This would help them become more financially stable. It would also make war between the countries much more difficult. The idea was interesting to other European countries as well. In 1951, France, West Germany, Belgium, Luxembourg, the Netherlands, and Italy signed the Treaty of Paris, creating the European Coal and Steel Community. These six countries would become the core of the EU.

In 1957, these same countries signed the Treaties of Rome, creating the European Economic Community. This combined their economies into a single European economy. In 1965, the Merger Treaty brought together a number of these treaty organizations. The organizations were joined under a common banner, known as the European Community. Finally, in 1992, the Maastricht Treaty was signed. This treaty defined the European Union. It gave a framework for expanding the EU's political role, particularly in the area of foreign and security policy. It would also replace national currencies with the euro. The next year, the treaty went into effect. At that time, the member countries included the original six plus another six who had joined during the 1970s and '80s.

In the following years, the EU would take more steps to form a single market for its members. This would make joining the union even more of an advantage. Three more countries joined during the 1990s. Another twelve joined in the first decade of the twenty-first century. As of 2012, six countries were waiting to join the EU.

The flag of the European Union.

His parents tell him that these families all decided to go back to their home country, but he knows it's not that simple. People on the street are saying the French government forced them to leave against their will. Some people seem to think that's a good thing; other people are angry. At this point, he's not sure what to think.

The kids that are gone now had darker skin than Jean-Pierre and his friends have. They dressed differently. He heard lots of stories about them. Some people said they were thieves. There have been lots of rumors.

And now the entire community is gone.

Jean-Pierre is growing up in one of the largest countries within the European Union (EU)—France. His proud nation is known for its unique culture and its long history of pride and resilience. Although France has endured plenty of wars and trials, this country has still come out strong. As one of the first nations to join the EU as a founding member, France is also known for its good relations with other European nations. It has been part of the eurozone, the European region that uses the euro as a monetary union, since the eurozone's beginning more than ten years ago. France has many strengths. But it also faces many challenges.

## THE ROMA IN FRANCE

In 2010, the French government made a bold move that upset many European nations. They **deported** thousands of Roma by forcing them to board airplanes and fly to other countries, such as Romania and Bulgaria. The French government claimed they were targeting illegal immigrants in general and not the Roma. Many people believed, however, that the French government had done something unjust.

Plenty of nations within the EU spoke up against France's actions. Despite this, France refused to change its attitude toward the Roma. The European Union even threatened to take legal action against France, stating that the French government had violated certain basic principals of the EU. For instance, **discrimination** is illegal under EU law. The French's defense to this was to cite another EU law: that all immigrants should hold citizenship in a member country of the EU before crossing borders into another EU country. Because many of these Roma were not legal citizens of any EU nation, the French government said their removal from France was justified.

However, it's not always that simple. The two countries to which the Roma are being deported—Bulgaria and Romania—are now member states of the EU. If the Roma being deported hold citizenship to one of these two nations, then they have the legal right to reside within French borders. France has countered this argument with the French law that states that immigrants cannot live in France for more than three months unless they find steady work. Unfortunately, discrimination often prevents the Roma from finding steady work that would allow them to stay in the country. Many become entertainers or street merchants.

Some of France's neighboring countries take great pride in their steps toward better treatment for the Roma. Spain, France's next-door neighbor to the west, is one nation that has become a model for integrating the Roma into their society. Other EU nations, however, support France's actions and have even followed in their footsteps, forcefully deporting Roma too.

## RELIGIOUS MINORITIES

Over 80 percent of France's population is **nominally** Roman Catholic, although religion doesn't play as big a role in the French people's lives as it once did. The second most-practiced religion is Islam, which includes somewhere between 5 and 10 percent of the population. The rest are Protestant, Jewish, or not affiliated with any religion.

# WHO ARE THE ROMA?

About a thousand years ago, groups of people migrated from northern India, spreading across Europe over the next several centuries. Though these people actually came from several different tribes (the largest of which were the Sinti and Roma), the people of Europe called them simply "Gypsies"—a shortened version of "Egyptians," since people thought they came from Egypt.

Europeans were frightened of these dark-skinned, non-Christian people who spoke a foreign language. Unlike the settled people of Europe, the Roma were wanderers, with no ties to the land. Europeans did not understand them. Stories and stereotypes grew up about the Gypsies, and these fanned the flames of prejudice and discrimination. Many of these same stories and stereotypes are still believed today.

Throughout the centuries, non-Gypsies continually tried to either assimilate the Gypsies or kill them. Attempts to assimilate the Gypsies involved stealing their children and placing them with other families; giving them cattle and feed, expecting them to become farmers; outlawing their customs, language, and clothing; and forcing them to attend school and church. In many ways the Roma of Europe were treated much as the European settlers treated the Native peoples of North America.

Many European laws allowed—or even commanded—the killing of Gypsies. A practice of "Gypsy hunting"—similar to fox hunting—was both common and legal in some parts of Europe. Even as late as 1835, a Gypsy hunt in Denmark "brought in a bag of over 260 men, women, and children." But the worst of all crimes against the Roma happened in the twentieth century, when Hitler's Third Reich sent them to concentration camps. As many as half a million Gypsies died in the Nazis' death camps.

Because of recent world events, those who practice Islam have not been seen in the best light. A certain sect of the Islamic faith helped created the conditions that led to the war in the Middle East. These **extremist** Muslims believe it is God's will that they fight back against Western nations, and they often use **terrorism** as their number-one weapon. These groups were responsible for the terrorist attacks against the United States on September 11, 2001, and they have also carried out violent and tragic attacks on European soil, including in Madrid and London.

For many people in the West (both the United States and Europe), Islam seems like a frightening religion that supports violence. Many people don't see the difference between terrorist extremists and peaceful Muslims. As a result, Muslims all over the world have become the victims of **hate crimes**. They face discrimination and **prejudice**.

Muslims praying.

# MUSLIMS IN THE EUROPEAN UNION

Muslims are people who follow Islam, a religion that grew from some of the same roots as Judaism and Christianity. "Islam" means "submission to God," and Muslims try to let God shape all aspects of their lives. They refer to God as Allah; their holy scriptures are called the Qur'an, and they consider the Prophet Muhammad to be their greatest teacher.

About 16 million Muslims live in the European Union—but their stories vary from country to country. Some Muslim populations have been living in Europe for hundreds of years. Others came in the middle of the twentieth century. Still others are recent refugees from the troubled Middle East. By 2020, the Muslim population in Europe is predicted to double. By 2050, one in five Europeans are likely to be Muslim, and by 2100, Muslims may make up one-quarter of Europe's people.

Not all Europeans are happy about these predictions. Negative stereotypes about Muslims are common in many EU countries. Some Europeans think all Muslims are terrorists. But stereotypes are dangerous!

When you believe a stereotype, you think that people in a certain group all act a certain way. "All jocks are dumb" is a stereotype. "All women are emotional" is another stereotype, and another is, "All little boys are rough and noisy." Stereotypes aren't true! And when we use stereotypes to think about others, we often fall into prejudice—thinking that some group of people aren't as good as others.

Fundamentalist Muslims want to get back to the fundamentals—the basics—of Islam. However, their definition of what's "fundamental" is not always the same as other Muslims'. Generally speaking, they are afraid that the influence of Western morals and values will be bad for Muslims. They believe that the laws of Islam's holy books should be followed literally. Many times, they are willing to kill for their beliefs—and they are often willing to die for them as well. Men and women who are passionate about these beliefs have taken part in violent attacks against Europe and the United States. They believe that terrorism will make the world take notice of them, that it will help them fight back against the West's power.

But most Muslims are not terrorists. In fact, most Muslims are law-abiding and hardworking citizens of the countries where they live. Some Muslims, however, believe that women should have few of the rights that women expect in most countries of the EU. This difference creates tension, since the EU guarantees women the same rights as men.

But not all Muslims are so conservative and strict. Many of them believe in the same "golden rule" preached by all major religions: "Treat everyone the way you want to be treated."

But despite this, hate crimes against Muslims are increasing across the EU. These crimes range from death threats and murder to more minor assaults, such as spitting and name-calling. Racism against Muslims is a major problem in many parts of the EU. The people of the European Union must come to terms with the fact that Muslims are a part of them now. Terrorism is the enemy to be fought—not Muslims.

France's large Muslim population—between 4 and 5 million people who identify as Muslim—makes it a very visible minority within French society. Their numbers are also increasing through immigration. On the one hand, this means that Muslims are becoming an increasingly important part of French society—and on the other hand, that fact scares some French people. They worry that the original "native French" culture will be swallowed up and lost. The French people are proud of their history; it's hard for them to balance their desire to preserve their unique identity with **tolerance** for new ideas and ways of living.

Despite France's efforts to deport "undesirable" residents, the EU's border laws mean that Roma, Muslims, and other groups of people will continue to come into France. As long as France is a member of the EU, it can do very little to regulate immigration. The French government doesn't like this. Many French people don't like it either. They are starting to wonder whether France should continue to be a part of the EU. They say they have their own problems—and they want their government to be able to take care of those problems instead of having to worry about immigrants.

## ECONOMIC SITUATION

Jean-Pierre's family, like many other French families in the twenty-first century, hasn't had it easy. His dad was laid off from his job last year. Fortunately for Jean-Pierre, education in France is free, so he can still go to school, but his home life has changed. His family has had to move to a smaller house in a neighborhood where there's more crime. They eat different foods than they used to. His mom still has a job, and now she works longer hours, while every day, his dad looks for work. Jean-Pierre feels like his parents are always tired and worried now. They're often in a bad mood, and they lose their tempers easily. When that happens, Jean-Pierre's entire family ends up cross and angry. It's easy, sometimes, for Jean-Pierre to feel angry at the Roma and the Muslims who live in their neighborhood. It would be nice to have someone to blame for his family's problems. It would be nice to think if the dark-skinned people in his community just went

## IMMIGRATION IN FRANCE

Immigration in all EU countries has increased significantly within the past decade. This is partially due to a policy put in place by the EU that any citizen of a member nation may travel freely to any other member country of the European Union. This law has meant that people within Europe move around more. Immigrants from eastern nations that recently joined the EU often move to the western nations. They are looking for jobs and better opportunities for their families, and they know that nations like France are wealthier and have more services to offer their residents.

France in particular often finds this law to be difficult to accept. Many French people are not happy that their neighbors may now have dark skin or worship God in a different way from the traditional French way. Minorities move freely across France's borders, only to be met with unfriendly treatment from French citizens.

away, then there would be enough jobs to go around—and things in his family could go back to normal.

In the early years of the twenty-first century, France, along with much of the rest of the world, went through a major **recession** (discussed more in chapter 3). This huge problem seemed to make all the country's other problems worse as well.

Other countries in a similar situation, however, have shown signs of slow, steady improvement. This is a good thing for France. With other countries'

economies improving, France will find it easier to get back on its own feet. The finances of the EU are woven together, so when one country does better, it's good for all the other member nations as well.

Although France faces many challenges, throughout its long and ancient history, it has dealt with many problems as serious or more serious than the ones it encounters in the twenty-first century. Hopefully, this proud past will give the nation strength and inspiration to overcome its modern-day problems.

France's currency is the euro.

A stone rooster perches on a medieval church in central France.

# 2

# FRANCE'S HISTORY AND GOVERNMENT

France has not always been the strong political power it is today. Throughout the ages, the land has been controlled by various groups and been the site of many bloody battles over its territories. Since prehistoric times, peoples have wanted to live in this fertile land.

## PREHISTORIC FRANCE

The first inhabitants of France, at around 15,000 BCE, were **hunter-gatherers** traveling from place to place in search of food. These Stone Age tribes left behind evidence of their existence in the form of cave paintings. These drawings, found throughout the Pyrenees but most notably in the

Lascaux caves, show the surprising technological advancement of the people of that time. Contrary to the stereotypes of cavemen as lumbering, unco-ordinated, almost monkey-like creatures, the amazing drawings on the cave walls show that the inhabitants of the area had fine motor skills and used forethought and creativity in planning their art. They also used tools like fine brushes

Roman ruins are scattered across France.

and paints to make these detailed drawings of animals and people.

By 6000 BCE, groups of settlers began to replace the migratory cultures in what is now France. These new peoples built a culture based on agriculture and farming, starting the process that would eventually change the country's landscape forever. Because this way of life was easier than how people had lived previously and could support more life, the population started to grow, increasing from four to five million by 1000 BCE. It was also around this time that metalworking was introduced, leading to the use of metals in such things as cooking pots and other tools.

Around 700 BCE, tribes from the north started invading the land. The largest group was the Celts, who spread throughout France, intermarrying and assimilating into the cultures that were already living there. Remnants of Celtic culture are still evident. For example, Gaul, a former name of what is now France, is derived from a Celtic word meaning "hero."

## THE ROMAN EMPIRE

In the last century BCE, the Roman Empire attacked what is now France. The Romans organized their new holdings much as they did the rest of the empire, setting in place a judicial system as well as administration. Cities sprang up as a transportation system was established and the economy expanded. These cities were based on Rome itself and contained such buildings as temples, public baths, and marketplaces, some of which still survive.

As the cities spread their Roman culture to the more rural areas, Latin gradually replaced Gaulish as the country's language. Religious practices changed as well, with Roman cults replacing the **Druids** and Celtic religions. In 100 CE, Christianity began to spread throughout France, at first only in the cities, which were each under the control of a bishop, but later taking root throughout the country. However, government officials discouraged and even repressed the practice of Christianity.

## DATING SYSTEMS AND THEIR MEANING

You might be accustomed to seeing dates expressed with the abbreviations BC or AD, as in the year 1000 BC or the year AD 1900. For centuries, this dating system has been the most common in the Western world. However, since BC and AD are based on Christianity (BC stands for Before Christ and AD stands for anno Domini, Latin for "in the year of our Lord"), many people now prefer to use abbreviations that people from all religions can be comfortable using. The abbreviations BCE (meaning Before Common Era) and CE (meaning Common Era) mark time in the same way (for example, 1000 BC is the same year as 1000 BCE, and AD 1900 is the same year as 1900 CE), but BCE and CE do not have the same religious overtones as BC and AD.

## THE FALL OF THE ROMAN EMPIRE

Germanic tribes like the Franks and the Alemanni began to take over areas of Roman Gaul in the third century. At first, this seemed like a good thing for the failing empire, as the flow of immigrants to the country provided a new workforce. However, not all of these groups were content to enter the land peacefully, and the Romans were forced to **ally** with tribes like the Franks, Burgundians, and Visigoths in the fifth century. While this prevented the immediate collapse of the empire, it weakened it, and gradually the Romans lost power.

Although Gaul was now under Germanic control, its Roman occupation would have a lasting impact on the country. It was the first time the country was united under one government. The Romans had founded many cities, including Paris. Modern-day highways are built on old Roman roads, leading to some confusion, as some roads seem to meander aimlessly through cities and the countryside. Even the French language is based on Latin, although there are some Germanic and other influences apparent.

## THE MIDDLE AGES

The immigration of these Germanic tribes into France marked the beginning of a period known as the Middle Ages. During the early period of this era, from about 350 to 1050, the state of the country declined; **literacy**, trade, and the legal system all deteriorated. However, not all aspects of life suffered. Many minorities achieved more rights during this era. Women were given the ability to maintain more control of property, and Jews, who had been persecuted under the Romans, were treated better under the Germanic kings.

Eventually, the Franks conquered the region that had once been Gaul and again gave the region a more centralized government. Led by Clovis, this group conquered much of present-day Germany and southeastern France. Clovis, realizing the importance of religion, converted to orthodox Christianity. At a time when most kings practiced Arianism, a type of Christianity not recognized by the Catholic Church, this made Clovis more agreeable to the pope, as well as making him more popular among his Christian subjects. His **precedent** led to centuries of rulers using Catholicism to aid them in their goals as leaders.

## THE REFORMATION

In 1517, Martin Luther began an attempt to reform the Catholic Church. This German theologian started a new belief system, Protestantism. In France, this new religion took many forms, the most popular one based on the teachings of John Calvin, a French **humanist**. The growing Protestant communities came to be known as Huguenots.

The government had mixed feelings about this new religion. Francis I, the monarch at the time, at first protected people suspected of being Protestants. As time went on, however, he eventually became more suspicious and less accepting. In the 1540s, thousands were tried and either put to death or sentenced to spend the rest of their lives rowing the galleys.

Christianity has played an important role in France's history.

At the same time, the Counter-Reformation traveled throughout France. This movement inspired reform of the existing Catholic Church, including the clergy and the development of new movements within the Church. Its goal was to again unite the nation under one faith—Catholicism.

In 1598, Henry IV issued the **Edict** of Nantes. This gave Protestants the right to practice their faith—under certain conditions. It also allowed them to have control of a few cities. However, this bill was so controversial that it was not registered for months. In the end, the edict did nothing to bring peace between the Protestants and Catholics. All it did was maintain the struggle at a less violent level.

## THE ENLIGHTENMENT

The 1700s brought an increase in France's literacy rate. This helped bring about the Enlightenment, a period of growth that brought new ideas and concepts to the country. This movement was led by the *philosophes*, a group of scientists and thinkers who worked toward reform. They wrote pamphlets and books, the best known of which is the *Encyclopédie*, an international best seller.

Although these people worked together, they all had very different ideas about politics, agreeing only on the fact that liberty and freedom were desirable. Some, like Charles Louis de Montesquieu, believed this was most easily brought about through protecting the rights of the people as individuals. Voltaire represented another group, those who thought a strong monarchy could be used to bring about freedom. Some of the more radical, like philosopher Jean Jacques Rousseau, believed a democracy should be established and the monarchy abolished altogether. These new thinkers were part of what led to the French Revolution.

## THE FRENCH REVOLUTION

Many factors caused the French Revolution. Among them was the fact that the king did not inspire much respect. Louis XV took little interest in the state of the country, leaving all the administrative decisions to his advisers. Instead, he seemed content to devote his attention to his many mistresses, especially the Marquise de Pompadour, who he refused to give up even when urged to by the court. Even after his death, the monarchy remained weak, with his son Louis XVI's only triumph being the American Revolution. Add this to the ideas spread by the Enlightenment and the hope for freedom inspired by the successful American Revolution, and the stage was set for change.

In 1788, the Estates-General decided to vote to give an equal vote to each estate, instead of basing it on the number of people in each estate. The Third Estate, which was formed from commoners and had the greatest number of representatives, saw this as an attempt to take power from them and give more to the First Estate (the clergy). After arguing over this issue for weeks, the Third Estate struck out on its own, forming a new parliament it called the National Assembly in June. The other two estates were invited to join, as long as they agreed to vote by head instead of estate, and a crisis was averted. However, this break from tradition made the king look bad as he searched for a way to gain control over the situation.

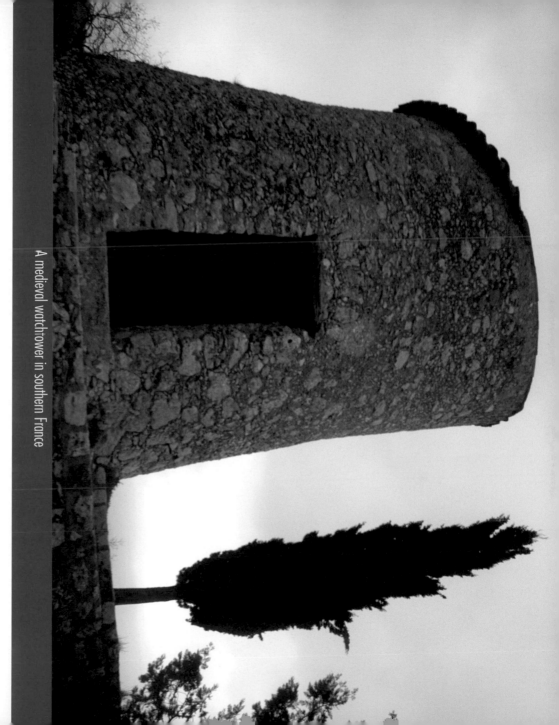
A medieval watchtower in southern France

Tensions deepened as a famine took hold in France. Peasants couldn't afford food since prices, especially of the cost of bread, kept rising and rising. Finally, desperate Parisians attacked the Bastille on July 14, 1789, a day now celebrated as a national holiday in France. The Bastille, an old prison, served as a symbol of the monarchy

The French nobility lived in manor houses like this one.

and everything the people wanted to put down. The French Revolution had begun.

The French Revolution caused more problems than had been anticipated. The government changed completely, and revolution became almost acceptable in the political arena. Because of this, a peaceful end was harder to reach than had been expected.

In 1789, France started its journey to recovery. To this end, the Declaration of the Rights of Man and of the Citizen was written. This was the beginning of a constitution, finished in 1791, that

EUROPEAN UNION—FRANCE

enforced a limited monarchy and put most authority in the hands of a **unicameral** legislature.

During this time, a mob of upset citizens forced the royal family to leave the palace at Versailles and remain in Paris, where the king was made to accept the reforms of the people. In 1791, the king and his family tried to escape, but were stopped at the border of France, where they were returned to Paris virtually prisoners.

A new legislative body, the National Convention, voted to end the monarchy in 1792. In its place was to be a republic. The king was tried and put to death in January 1793.

Not all was peaceful among the members of the National Convention. In 1793, Maximillian Robespierre and his following of radical **Jacobeans** took over the parliament and started the Reign of Terror, a time meant to force citizens to help the republic. Over a quarter of a million people were arrested, and more than 30,000 guillotined, often for the most trivial of reasons or because they were alleged to have worked against the republic. Eventually, they had alienated the remainder of France so much that Robespierre and his advisers were executed, ending the Reign of Terror.

For the first time since the Revolution, a moderate government was put in place. A new convention worked to keep the accomplishments of the Revolution, while keeping an event like the Terror from ever happening again. To this extent, a **bicameral** legislature was developed as well as an executive branch consisting of five members known as the Directory. Although this system worked for a while, it was ultimately unsuccessful,

setting the stage for the next period in France's history: the rule of Napoleon Bonaparte.

## NAPOLEON BONAPARTE

In 1799, Napoleon and his troops attacked the government, putting in place one of their own devising, called the Consulate. It consisted of Bonaparte and two others, but Napoleon was the one really in charge. After reforming the government, he declared himself emperor, and the country was back to where it had been before the Revolution.

At its height, Napoleon's First Empire went from Poland to Spain, as well as being allied with Russia, Prussia, and Austria. However, it didn't last long as countries used to independence rebelled. Perhaps one of Napoleon's biggest mistakes and one that led to his downfall was his attack of Russia in 1812, a mistake later repeated by Adolf Hitler during World War II. Caught in the middle of a Russian winter, Napoleon's troops quickly ran out of food and supplies; trucks were unable to get to them. The French troops never came into armed conflict with the Russians—the native troops retreated, burning any towns and cities that might have proved useful to the French. After thousands of his soldiers died from starvation and exposure, Napoleon was forced to admit defeat without reaching his destination of Moscow. By 1814, Napoleon was forced to abdicate his throne when armies invaded France. He was exiled to the island of Elba.

The year after, Napoleon tried to return. He came back to France, and for a short time, known as the Hundred Days, Napoleon gathered the people to him with talk of a more left-wing regime. However, at the Battle of Waterloo, Napoleon was defeated again. This time he was exiled to the island of Saint Helena, where he died in 1821.

## The Industrial Revolution

Unlike Great Britain, where the change from household industries to factories seemed to occur almost overnight, France's Industrial Revolution was more gradual. For many years, France was behind countries like Germany and Britain. Not only had France just gotten out of decades of revolutions, but it did not have as big a population growth as did other countries. One of the reasons for a lag in population growth was that the peasant class, almost extinct in other European countries, was still around. Because they were poor, family size was limited, leading to a lower birthrate. Therefore, there was less demand for more goods, because there were less people to ask for them.

The Industrial Revolution started in the textile industry, as it did in many other countries. However, in the 1840s, the railway industry brought a boom throughout the economy. This also increased a demand for mining and metal ores to make rails. The Revolution eventually led to the development of a middle class, who worked mainly in small shops and professional jobs.

## World War I

France's involvement in World War I began in 1914, when German troops came through Belgium, looking to take control of Paris and defeat the French troops trying to retake Alsace-Lorraine from Germany. France's success in keeping the Germans from accomplishing their goals may have been the factor that kept the other side from winning quickly. Instead, a stalemate resulted that lasted for years, with neither side gaining much territory. The only result was the loss of thousands of lives.

The Treaty of Versailles, which ended the war, dictated the terms of peace. France regained control of Alsace-Lorraine, and Germany was forced to pay *reparations* for the war. Germany also had to agree to demilitarize the area between France and Germany known as the Rhineland, which France could occupy until 1935.

World War I led to another decline in France's birthrate as millions of men returned home wounded or, worse, didn't return home at all. Immigrants came into the country to take the jobs left behind by the lost soldiers. During the war, women had been allowed to work in factories, but were now pushed out of their jobs to make room for veterans. There were also economic losses as the area that Germany had taken over contained more than half of the steel and coal industries. Coupled with the economic cost of the war itself, debt increased and the value of the franc weakened.

In 1928, France joined the League of Nations in an attempt to stave off another war. However, this organization was weak and had no real power, partly because the United States refused to join.

French veterans remember the role the nation played in the world wars.

## WORLD WAR II

In 1939, after numerous violations by Germany of the Treaty of Versailles, and despite the League of Nations' attempts at **appeasement**, war was declared on that country. At first, France maintained its neutrality. Then, in 1940, Hitler attacked France. Unlike what had happened in World War I, this was a decisive victory for Germany, and France became an occupied country.

In 1918, France signed an **armistice** saying that they would demobilize their armed forces, basically giving over the northern two-thirds of the country to Germany. Despite ceding to all of Germany's demands, the country still suffered. Thousands of forced laborers worked in Germany, and the country was forced to give money to help support the German war effort. In 1942, Germany took control over the remainder of France, resulting in a French puppet government.

Vichy, the government at the time, was almost as bad as the Germans. While not actively involved in **genocide**, anti-Semitism was rampant, and Jews were forced to give up their jobs and property. Some Jews were sent to Germany, where they were placed in death camps.

Although most people supported the French government at first, people began resisting German control. Charles de Gaulle, the former undersecretary of war, escaped to Paris, where he formed a government in exile. Groups of people fought against the Germans, sabotaging the war effort and secretly communicating with de Gaulle.

France was liberated in 1944 after Allied troops landed at Normandy. A new provisional government, led by de Gaulle, assumed power.

## FRANCE AND THE EUROPEAN UNION

France was a founding member of the European Union (EU), which was established by the Maastricht Treaty in 1991, which went into effect in 1993 after the treaty was ratified by all member nations. The country had its six-month term as president during the last half of 2008.

As well as helping to put in place the EU, now one of the most influential organizations in the world, France also founded many of the preceding organizations and treaties, such as the European Coal and Steel Community (ECSC) and the European Community (EC).

## FRANCE'S GOVERNMENT TODAY

France's modern government consists of a republic led by a president, much like the United States. The current form of government was established with a new constitution in 1958, one that gave more power to the president and less to parliament.

The president is elected by popular vote; there is no **electoral college** as in the United States. The president is the head of state and of the country, but he must appoint a prime minister who takes over the task of controlling the government. The legislative branch of the government is bicameral; parliament is made up of the National Assembly and the Senate, which has slightly less influence. There is also the Constitutional Council, a judicial branch of the government that supervises elections and decides the constitutionality of laws.

Amendments to the constitution may come about in many different ways. The president can propose an amendment, or the government or members of parliament may request one. However the amendment is proposed, it must have the approval of both branches of the parliament and be approved in a referendum.

There are three levels of local government: communes, departments, and regions. Communes are the smallest and can range in size from one small village to a piece of a larger city. Then there are departments, most of them named after the geographical area where they are. These departments make up the regions, the largest piece of the local governments. No matter what the size, all of these have their own elected legislative and executive branches.

A medieval castle off the coast of Antibes reminds modern French citizens of their past.

Vacationers from around the world flock to Nice's warm beaches and fancy restaurants.

# 3 CHAPTER

# THE ECONOMY

All countries within the EU have very close financial ties. If one country is doing well, it will have a positive effect on the countries with which it trades. A successful country will stimulate the economy in a less successful region. However, if one country is doing poorly, it will have a negative effect on the countries with which it trades. If many countries are beginning to have economic problems, they will pull down even more countries with them. This is the case in Europe today.

Unlike some of the newer nations to have joined the EU, however, France has many economic strengths on which to build. Just as it has long and proud political history, it also has a history of strong finances.

## FRANCE'S ECONOMIC HISTORY

While French industry consisted of mainly farms and small businesses until the 1940s, after World War II, the government set in place a plan designed to modernize the economy. These reforms consisted of nationalizing different industries, including energy production, the banking system, and many factories and other manufacturing fields. This, along with France's induction into the EC—the forerunner of the EU—led to a period of economic growth in the past twenty-five years. Early in the twenty-first century, France boasted the world's fifth-strongest economy, behind only the

France's medieval castles attract visitors from around the world, making tourism an important factor in the nation's economy.

United States, Japan, Germany, and the United Kingdom.

As of 2011, France's **gross domestic product (GDP)** was equivalent to 2.21 trillion American dollars. Per capita income is US$35,000. Though this may seem like a lot of money, not everyone earns this much. This is an average figure—the average amount an average French citizen earns in a year; many people earn far below this amount, while others earn much more.

## ENTRANCE INTO THE EU

The creation of the EU put in place a single market in Europe for producers to sell their goods and services. Though this has allowed people, capital, and goods to move freely throughout Europe, there have been some downfalls. French businesses, used to protection by trade barriers, have become more competitive in order to survive in the wider marketplace.

The formation of the EU also brought about the adoption of the euro. This common currency makes it even easier for people and goods to travel from one country to another.

## SOCIALISM: HOW MUCH CONTROL SHOULD THE GOVERNMENT HAVE?

Various French governments have tried different variations of government control of the economy. In 1982, François Mitterrand, then the president of the country, attempted to **nationalize** most of the economy. At the height of this socialist plan, the state owned thirteen of twenty of the major corporations in France.

Since then, the government has begun to encourage limited privatization of businesses. Now France tends toward a mixed economy, a system in which both government and private sectors share control of various industries.

Although there is some private ownership of goods and services in the economy, the government is still involved, using its influence to make sure the economy is growing and stable. France used fiscal policies, such as cutting taxes and increasing government spending, to increase demand for goods by giving people more money to spend and therefore encouraging the economy to grow. However, this policy often results in a budget deficit, with the government spending more than it takes in, and in 2003, France received a warning from the EU to restrain its government spending and keep under the 3 percent budget deficit limit the EU has set in place. In the last few years, France's debt has been as much as 7.5 percent of GDP in 2009.

## TAXES AND OTHER INCOMES

The French government gets income from many sources, including taxes. Things like sales tax and income tax provide the government with money. There is also a wealth tax in France, which those with assets worth more than 800,000 euro must pay. All in all, France is one of the most heavily taxed nations in the EU.

A large part of the GDP comes from government expenditure. Social security, the wages of government employees, debt service on the national debt, and investment all contribute to the money people make from the federal government.

## THE LABOR FORCE

The structure of the economy has changed drastically in recent years. In the 1950s, most French workers had jobs in agriculture or industry. Now, however, the **service sector** is the most popular, employing 80 percent of France's labor force of 29.56 million people. The highest numbers of new jobs are in the education, health, and public administration fields.

## ECONOMIC SECTORS

France is the EU's leading producer of agricultural goods, with more than 48.4 million acres (19.6 million hectares) used for farming. The country produces dairy products, beef, wheat, oilseeds, fruits and vegetables, and wine.

The reason France is able to produce so many different products is because the country is so well suited to agriculture. There is fertile soil, plentiful rain, and a long growing season. The variety comes from regional differences in climate—in the northwest, where it is cooler and wetter, there are grasslands for cattle to graze on, while in the Mediterranean region, where it is warm and dry, it is easy to grow various types of grapes.

The Common Agricultural Policy (CAP) was put in place in 1957 with the creation of the European Economic Community (EEC). This created a system of common prices across what is now the EU, leading to greater agricultural production and helping many farmers improve their incomes. Because France is the leading agricultural country in the EU, it benefits the most from these funds.

France also is a mining country, the second-largest producer of iron ore in Western Europe. This was once a major source of employment, but production decreased when it was discovered that French iron has many impurities. However, other metals and minerals—such as uranium, aluminum, salt, gypsum, tungsten, and sulfur—are still mined. Coal is also mined, although on a much smaller scale than during the turn of the twentieth century. There are also stone quarries that provide such materials as sand, gravel, stone, and clay.

Manufacturing is another major industry in France. It accounts for the main source of income through exports and produces such goods as food products, automobiles, airplanes, ships, trains, machinery, chemicals, and textiles. The country is well known for its innovations in the transportation sectors; the French TGV (*Train á Grande Vitesse* or Train of Great Speed) is one of the world's fastest passenger trains.

People from all over the world come to France to visit, making tourism an important part of the service sector. France is the most visited nation in the world, with more than 75 million people coming to see this beautiful and historic nation. The French themselves travel around their own country, taking advantage of the five-week paid vacation all French workers must receive, to experience a different part of France.

France's fertile farmland

# TRANSPORTATION

France enjoys a well-maintained network of highways, railroads, and waterways. The country's dense system of roads make it home to one of the best transportation systems in the world. It was the first country in the EU to have fast railroads available for passengers. The Metro systems in the cities, most notably Paris, are easy to use and very comfortable.

Paris is the center of the transportation system. It is home to a major airport—Charles de Gaulle—

and all of France's major roads and waterways lead from the city. Recently, however, efforts have been made to connect other larger cities while skipping Paris.

water transport of goods has decreased in the last decades as other alternatives, such as air transportation, have become cheaper and easier. There are many seaports in France, such as those at Marseille and Le Havre, which are the entry points for the country's imports of petroleum.

## ENERGY

France has few natural energy resources of its own, relying mainly on imported petroleum. While the country was able to mine coal during the Industrial Revolution, this power source was quickly outdated as gasoline developed, and gasoline is a scarce commodity in France. In 1973, the oil crisis showed the pitfalls of depending on foreign oil, and the government started developing alternative energy sources.

France found that it could use nuclear power to make its own energy, thereby reducing the amount it needed to import from other countries. France's nuclear power plants produce about 75.2 percent of its power; after the United States, France is the largest producer of nuclear power plants. While this has met with few protests, not all attempts to harness this type of power have been successful. In southeastern France, a plant was closed in 1998 after

France has more than 5,300 miles (8,500 kilometers) of navigable rivers and canals, making it the longest system of water transportation in Europe. Because most of these canals were built in the 1800s and today's large ships cannot fit,

## QUICK FACTS: THE ECONOMY OF FRANCE

**Gross Domestic Product (GDP):** US$2.214 trillion (2011 est.)

**GDP per capita:** US$35,000 (2011 est.)

**Industries:** machinery, chemicals, automobiles, metallurgy, aircraft, electronics; textiles, food processing; tourism

**Agriculture:** wheat, cereals, sugar beets, potatoes, wine grapes; beef, dairy products; fish

**Export commodities:** machinery and transportation equipment, aircraft, plastics, chemicals, pharmaceutical products, iron and steel, beverages

**Export partners:** Germany 16.4%, Italy 8.2%, Belgium 7.7%, Spain 7.6%, UK 6.8%, US 5.1%, Netherlands 4.2% (2010)

**Import commodities:** machinery and equipment, vehicles, crude oil, aircraft, plastics, chemicals

**Import partners:** Germany 19.3%, Belgium 11.4%, Italy 8%, Netherlands 7.5%, Spain 6.8%, China 5.1%, UK 5% (2010)

**Currency:** euro

**Currency exchange rate:** US$1 = 0.7107 euro (March, 2012)

*Note: All figures are from 2011 unless otherwise noted.*
*Source: www.cia.gov, 2012.*

technical problems and safety concerns, along with protests from various environmental groups.

Not all of France's electricity comes from nuclear power; the country also uses hydroelectric and thermal power. France produces more energy than it needs, exporting the excess to the countries around it, such as the UK, Italy, and Switzerland.

## ECONOMIC PROBLEMS

Even while France had a strong economy, the country still had many problems. One of these was the high unemployment rate. From the mid-1970s, the number of people without jobs had been consistently over 10 percent, falling slightly to 9 percent in 2002 and then jumping back to 9.8 percent in 2012. While some unemployment is usually unavoidable, the rate of full employment is considered to be around 5 percent—half that of France. France has taken many measures to lower unemployment, but with limited success; among these efforts was a law that reduced the workweek from thirty-nine to thirty-five hours, which means that more workers would be needed to accomplish the same tasks, creating more jobs).

Because the economy is not growing very fast, it is getting harder and harder for France to maintain its welfare system, which has traditionally been extremely generous to its citizens. France is finding it necessary to reform this system, delicately balancing the benefits each person may receive with a solution that is agreeable to the public.

Prior to the world's economic downfall, France was going through several reforms that seemed to be improving its economy. Former French president Nicolas Sarkozy brought about much of this change. He assumed office in 2007 as president, and he immediately set out to improve working conditions. Under his leadership, laws were passed to stimulate economic growth.

But Sarkozy's high hopes didn't work out as the French people had hoped. Although France is still said to have one of the largest economies in the world, growth rate dropped beginning in 2009. Its unemployment percentage is staggeringly high for a developed nation such as France. Those who manage to find jobs are facing involuntary cutbacks of both pay and hours, making it harder to live comfortably. In the 2012 French presidential election, François Hollande defeated Sarkozy, partially as a result of anger about cuts in social programs made by Sarkozy's government.

The EU is working hard to help its members rise above the recession. France will likely face more hard times, however, before it can find its way out of the economic crisis.

A young French boy fishing in Antibes

# 4

# FRANCE'S PEOPLE AND CULTURE

France is home to nearly 66 million people (as of 2012), making it the second most populated nation in Europe. While many people live here, it is also the largest nation in Western Europe, meaning that the population density is still less than in most European nations, with 297 people per square mile (118 people per square kilometer).

## ETHNICITIES

Although most people in the country speak French, they have varied ethnic backgrounds. Hundreds of years of invading groups have left their mark, including the Romans, Celts, and Franks, from whom the name France comes.

The French government has tried hard to *assimilate* minorities and has come a long way from the French Revolution when less than half of the people spoke French. After the Revolution, in an attempt to find unity, the government declared that if a person lived in France, they were French. This was part of the government's effort to make a nation based on a common language. This worked until the formation of the EU, which forced France for the first time to acknowledge and offer rights to minorities.

Many ethnic minorities are descended from ancient peoples and live on the same land their ancestors have inhabited for centuries. For example, in the northern part of France live a group called the Flemings, who live around the town of Dunkerque. They speak mainly a *dialect* of Dutch and have assimilated without protest into French culture. On the other hand, the Bretons, who have Celtic blood and live in Brittany, seek to have their own culture and way of life. To this end they differentiate themselves from the French by incorporating their Celtic heritage into their lives and setting up schools in their own language.

Immigrants from all over the world make up approximately 7.5 percent of France's population. The largest immigrant group is from North Africa, including the Islamic nations of Algeria, Morocco, and Tunisia. There are more than 4 million Muslims in France, many from Africa or Turkey and who live in France's cities. This has led to much debate as people argue over whether or not traditional Islamic head coverings should be allowed in school. In 2004, a law was passed forbidding schoolchildren from wearing religious symbols; many Muslims felt the law was targeting them. In 2011, wearing veils over the face became illegal. It is now against the law for Muslim women to cover their faces in public.

## LANGUAGE

French is the official language of France. The language is a dialect of the ancient *langue d'oïl*, which originated in what is now northern France. Other, regional languages are spoken as well, the most widespread of which is Occitan, the *langue d'oc* (Languedoc), which is spoken mainly in southern France. Almost 6 million speak *Provençal*, the major dialect. However, most people speak mainstream French as well.

Other languages include German in the region of Alsace; Breton in Brittany; Catalan, and Basque, which are based in the Pyrenees; Flemish, which is based on Dutch; and Corse, an Italian dialect spoken on the island of Corsica. Many of France's immigrants also speak their native languages, most notably Arabic and Turkish.

## RELIGION IN FRANCE

The most popular religion in France is Roman Catholicism, with more than 80 percent of the population claiming to practice this faith. However, while many identify with this religion and its culture, only a few—about 5 percent—actively practice it.

Islam is France's second-largest faith, with about 5 percent of the population Muslim. There are also some Protestants, although these are a minority. Protestants fled France in the sixteenth and seventeenth centuries because of persecution

from the Catholics; not many returned. There is also a small Jewish minority. However, more than 10 percent of the French people claim to have no religion at all.

The government supported both Christianity and Judaism until the beginning of the twentieth century. In 1905, church and state were officially separated. Because many people opposed the

Christianity is important to France's history and culture.

Catholic Church and their control over schools and the educational system, the government was forbidden to pay public funds to any religious official or clergy. Therefore, the state cannot officially recognize any religion.

## EDUCATION

Basic schooling is guaranteed for all French citizens. Students must attend school from ages six to sixteen, and all schools are free. Universities are also free to those students who qualify. There is also an extensive system of private schools, many controlled by the Catholic Church. One out of six children attend these schools.

Education starts out with two or three years of preschool, which is optional. Students go on to a primary, or elementary school until they are eleven. After the *collège*, or middle school, which students attend until they are fifteen, they go on to *lyceé*, or high school. Here teens have a choice. There are general schools, which are much like those in the United States, offering a well-rounded education in all the subjects. Students attend these general schools for three years, ending with a nationwide exam. If students pass this exam, they earn the *baccalauréate* degree needed to enter a university. This is a hard exam; only two-thirds of those who take it pass, and the others must take it over again. Students can also decide to go to a technical or vocational school and earn a professional certificate/diploma after one to three years.

The system of universities is expanding, adding new colleges apart from the general, traditional university. One such type is the technological institutes, or *instituts universitaires de technologie*. They specialize in such fields as engineering and other technology-related majors. Community colleges have also developed in smaller cities and towns.

Besides colleges and universities, there are graduate schools, called *grandes écoles*. These are extremely hard to get into; applicants must pass competitive exams.

## SPORTS

The French people are very active, loving physical activity of all kinds. While professional sports like soccer (called *le foot*) and bicycle racing are extremely popular, many people belong to sports clubs where they play for fun. The most widespread of these clubs allow members to play soccer, tennis, basketball, or *boules*.

The Tour de France is the world's most famous bicycle race. Each year such legends as Lance Armstrong gather to compete for the prize. The French Open, one of tennis's Grand Slam events, attracts visitors from around the world to the clay courts of Roland-Garros Stadium in Paris.

# FRENCH FOOD

It is a not uncommon to see French people sitting at sidewalk cafés, enjoying a cup of coffee or Orangina, a popular French drink, while they watch the passersby or read the paper. These small restaurants are all over France, pointing to the emphasis the culture places on food.

France is famous for its food; the country has many regional dishes that can be found nowhere else in the world. Some of the more popular foods that have become internationally known include

France is famous for its wine and cheese.

quiches; crêpes; bouillabaisse, a fish soup; and pâté de foie gras, a spread made of goose livers. French bread is also known for its taste; most people go every day to *boulangeries* to get fresh baked goods.

Unlike Americans, whose largest meal of the day tends to be eaten in the evening, the French eat a small breakfast, a big lunch, and a small dinner. For special occasions, however, huge, multi-course meals are served, lasting from around 8 P.M. until sometimes very early in the morning. These elaborate dinners consist of appetizers, one or two main courses, a salad, fruits and cheeses, and then dessert. Of course, various types of wine are served throughout the meal.

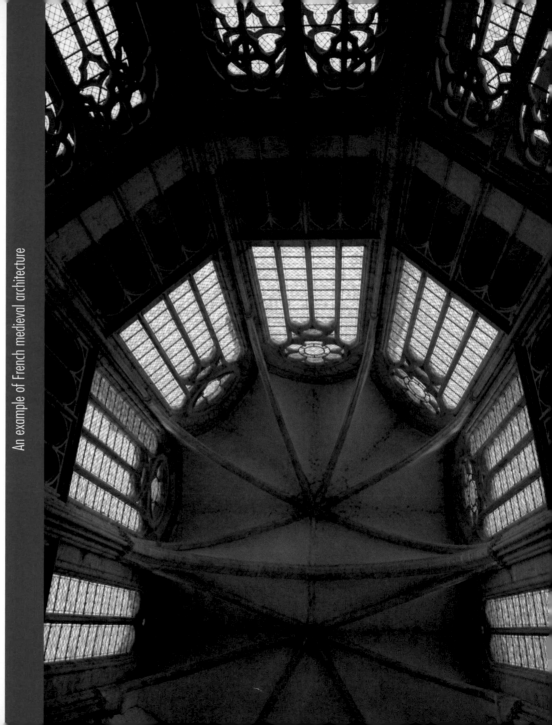

An example of French medieval architecture

## FESTIVALS AND HOLIDAYS

Because much of French culture is based on Roman Catholicism, many of the holidays celebrated have a religious base. Christmas and Easter are celebrated much as they are in the United States. However, a festival with a uniquely French flavor is Mardi Gras, or Fat Tuesday. This is the day before Lent (the forty days preceding Easter) and marks the end of the Carnival season. Parades, music, costumes, and food highlight the festivities, as people rush to celebrate before the traditional season of fasting and prayer.

The national holiday in France is Bastille Day on July 14. This celebrates the fall of the Bastille and the success of the common people in the French Revolution. There are many regional festivals, celebrating everything from food to film and from music to another successful harvest.

## THE ARTS: ARCHITECTURE, PAINTING, MUSIC, AND LITERATURE

France has produced many famous artists, as well as developing whole movements of painting. One such style is Impressionism, a movement of the late nineteenth and early twentieth centuries. The movement got its name from Claude Monet's painting *Impressionist Sunrise*. Although he refused to call himself an Impressionist, one of the first practitioners of the technique was Édouard Manet. Pierre Auguste Renoir is one of Impressionism's most famous artists.

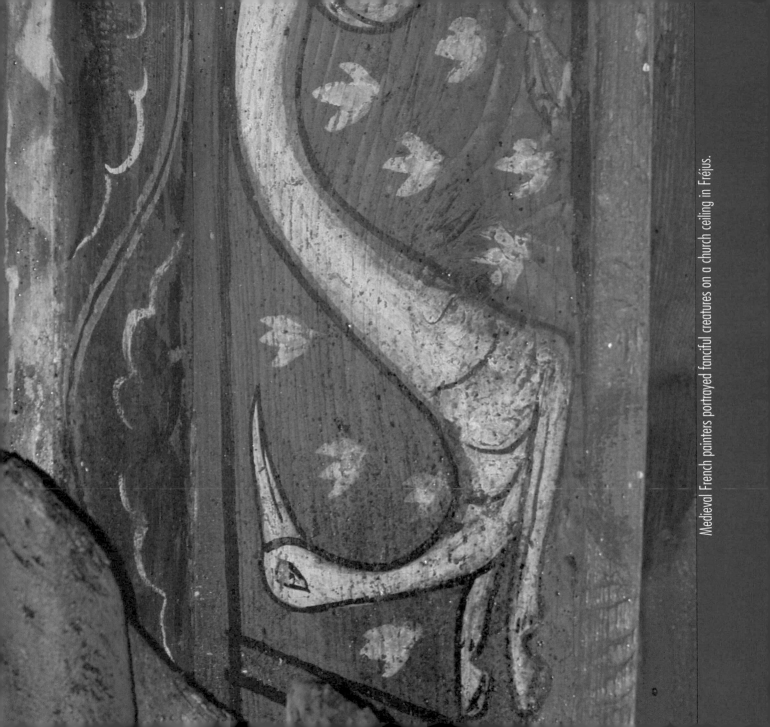

Medieval French painters portrayed fanciful creatures on a church ceiling in Fréjus.

However, French painters have won prestige throughout history, from Baroque artists like Georges de la Tour and Claude Lorrain to Romantic painters like Eugène Delacroix. In the twentieth century, Henri Matisse, Pierre Bonnard, and Marcel Duchamp became famous for their modern works.

Painting is not the only art form at which the French excel. The country is rife with examples of great architecture, the earliest examples being its Gothic churches, built between the twelfth and fifteenth centuries. The palace of Versailles is a great example of the luxury of the neoclassical era, and, of course, the Eiffel Tower shows the talent of the nineteenth-century Charles Garnier.

Since the eleventh century, French musicians have been singing of noble deeds and quests in the form of *chansons de geste*. Throughout history France has continued this musical tradition, creating new forms of music and raising famous composers. In the 1300s, composer Guillaume de Machaut developed the polyphonic form of music, or the idea that music could have more than one part. Famous French musicians and composers include Georges Bizet, Camille Saint-Saëns, Gabriel Fauré, and Claude Debussy. The French continue to enjoy music, and newer forms are popular today, including rock and pop hits.

French literature has been world famous for centuries. Writers such as Marcel Proust and Albert Camus continue to be popular. The country is also home to many books for a younger audience; children all over the world read *The Little Prince* by Antoine de Saint Exupéry.

Lavender field in Provence, France.

# 5 LOOKING TO THE FUTURE

When Jean-Pierre listens to the adults in his life talk about the future, he starts to feel worried. His country faces so many problems right now. He wonders what things will be like by the time he's ready to look for work. But his family has reason to feel hopeful.

## ECONOMIC IMPROVEMENT

One day, Jean-Pierre's dad came home and shouted, "Finally, I have my old job back!" His father explained that the economy was doing a bit better, and his old boss could now afford to take him back. He wouldn't be working for the same pay, but at least he'd be making something—and at least he'd have a steady job!

Jean-Pierre's family is one of the lucky ones. Plenty of other people in France remain without jobs as they wait for the economy to recover. No one can be sure when that will happen, but plenty of countries in the EU are already showing signs of recovery. France, Germany, and Italy all achieved some positive growth during 2012, which was a good sign.

No country in the EU has yet reached where it was before the recession—but some are getting close. In the first half of 2012, France had another 1 percent to go, while Italy and Germany were both a little more than 2 percent away from where they were prior to the recession. Experts predicted that the economy would continue to improve very slowly, although no one could really be sure. It could take a very long time before the economy is stable again. The shape of France's future will depend in large part in how the entire world's economy does in the years to come.

## ENVIRONMENTAL DEVELOPMENTS

Meanwhile, people in France have other concerns for the future. The environment is one of the biggest.

Human beings' current lifestyles are taking a toll on our planet. Climate change, pollution, and diminishing resources are all major problems the entire Earth must face. The European Union takes these challenges very seriously. It has passed a *resolution* that by 2020, all members of the EU should be getting 20 percent of all their energy from clean, *renewable* sources. This is a huge goal to reach, and some nations are doing better than others at making progress toward it.

France has come to rely on nuclear power over the past few decades. In fact, almost 80 percent of all its energy is drawn from nuclear sources, while only about 10 percent comes from renewable energy sources. Almost all of this comes from *hydroelectric* power, a very clean source, but France will need to learn to rely less on nuclear energy and more on other renewable sources like wind. The 2011 earthquake and tsunami in Japan, with the destruction that has caused to Japanese nuclear reactors, has made many French people worried that their nation depends so much on nuclear power for their energy needs.

Meanwhile, however, the past few years' economic problems have changed the priorities of many nations, including France. Sometimes the environment doesn't seem as important as jobs, and the search for safer, renewable energy sources has often been put on the backburner while the country tries to find ways to improve living conditions for its citizens. As the world looks at Japan's conditions after the 2011 earthquake and tsunami, though, many people are realizing that a stable economy does very little good in the face of

France uses dams such as this one to produce hydroelectric power.

environmental disaster; at the very foundation of all nations' economies, is the need to protect our planet. Hopefully, this is a lesson the world will remember.

## CULTURAL CONCERNS

The French government does not recognize minorities. This is both a good and bad thing. In the eyes of the law, every citizen is equal, and discrimination is unconstitutional. However, this also means that no specific laws or policies protect minorities the way they do in the United States. Members of minority groups find it very hard to preserve their

culture because they have no legal support. In the eyes of the government, integration of all cultures is the most important goal. Minority groups are forced to conform to the cultural standards of the entire nation, rather than having their unique cultural and religious traditions protected. Meanwhile, since minorities don't legally exist, it's hard for human rights **advocates** to find a way to communicate with the government about discriminatory practices that affect minority communities.

On the other side of the equation, people whose families who have lived in France for centuries worry that France's ancient culture will inevitably become "watered down" by so many French residents who come from very different cultural backgrounds around the world.

The world recognizes that the traditional French culture is indeed something valuable and precious. Plenty of international travelers visit France each year to experience its unique culture and learn about its history. As a result, tourism is one of the big preservers of French culture. Because so many people want to discover what is uniquely French, tourists actually help protect the traditional French culture.

## SOCIAL WELFARE

Many French people are worried about their personal futures in a changing economic climate. With the country facing serious financial challenges, the government is looking at cutting social welfare programs that many French people take for granted. Former president Sarkozy cut pension plans and insisted that the legal retirement age needed to be raised. Many French people were furious. These tensions have only added to the strained atmosphere in France. Sarkozy lost the 2012 presidential election to François Hollande due in part to his government's cutting social welfare programs.

## FRANCE'S PLACE IN THE EU

Although France has always been a leading member of the European Nations ever since the EU's foundation, as France moves into the second decade of the twenty-first century, the world won-ders if France will be able to think in terms of what is good for the EU as a whole, rather than from the perspective of what is good for France only.

One of the biggest challenges for France is the EU's policy of open borders. In April 2011, France asked the EU to change the border treaty that permits passport-free travel through Europe. The unrest in northern Africa in 2011 meant that a flood of immigrants fled from Africa into Europe, looking for safer lives and better living conditions. France doesn't believe these people should be allowed to enter the EU. It criticized Italy for granting temporary residency permits to some 20,000 Tunisian migrants who arrived in Italy after the North African nation's dictator was overthrown in January 2011. Once these immigrants were in Italy, France pointed out, they would be able to pass across the border into France (and most Tunisians did in fact want to get to France, where many had relatives already living). France stopped a train carrying Tunisian immigrants from Italy at the French border and sent back everyone who could not prove they could support themselves financially.

The immigration issue is a key factor in France's future, but other nations also accuse France of taking advantage of other European nations' weaker economies in order to build up France's economy. By 2012, several French companies had taken over weaker companies in other EU nations.

One of the big issues in the EU is similar to one that the United States faces as well: who should have more power, the central government (the EU in Europe, or Washington, D.C., in the United States) or the individual members (the

France is working hard to preserve the country's natural beauty by tackling its environmental issues.

nations of Europe or the states of the United States? This issue becomes obvious when smaller issues arise. In the United States, it came to a head in the 1800s over the issue of slavery, causing the Civil War, but it continues to be an important question whenever states don't agree on a particular issue, such as same-sex marriage or abortion rights. The smaller issues in Europe are different (they have to do with the Roma, with immigration, and with money), but the big issue is very much the same.

France's future will be shaped by the answers it finds to this question: Will it be able to unite its power with the EU the way America's states try to work together as a single nation—or will it act as a separate state, concerned only for its own interests?

# TIME LINE

| | |
|---|---|
| 15,000 BCE | The first inhabitants settle in France. |
| 6000 BCE | Agricultural-based cultures settle in France. |
| 700 BCE | Tribes from the north start invading the area. |
| 1 BCE | The Roman Empire attacks what is now France. |
| 100 CE | Christianity begins to spread throughout France. |
| 350–1050 | The country suffers a period of decline. |
| 751 | Pepin the Short declares himself monarch. |
| 800 | Pope Leo crowns Charlemagne head of the Roman Empire. |
| 1152 | Henry II, the king of England, the duke of Normandy, marries Eleanor of Aquitaine, making her the first woman to sit on the thrones of two countries: England and France. |
| 1517 | Martin Luther begins an attempt to reform the Catholic Church. |
| 1540s | Many Protestants and suspected Protestants are tried and either put to death or sentenced to spend the rest of their lives rowing the galleys. |
| 1598 | Henry IV issues the Edict of Nantes. |
| July 14, 1789 | Parisians attack the Bastille. |
| 1789 | The Declaration of the Rights of Man and of the Citizen is written. |
| 1793 | The king is tried and put to death. |
| 1793 | Maximillian Robespierre and his following of radical Jacobeans take over the parliament and the Reign of Terror begins. |
| 1799 | Napoleon and his troops attack the government and replace it with the Consulate. |
| 1814 | Napoleon abdicates his throne and is exiled. |
| 1815 | Napoleon returns to France and is defeated at the Battle of Waterloo. |
| 1821 | Napoleon dies in exile. |
| 1905 | Church and state are officially separated. |
| 1914 | France enters World War I. |
| 1918 | France signs an armistice saying that they would demobilize their armed forces. |
| 1928 | France joins the League of Nations. |
| 1940 | Hitler attacks France. |
| 1944 | Allied troops liberate France. |
| 1982 | President François Mitterrand attempts to nationalize most of the economy. |
| 1991 | France becomes a founding member of the EU. |
| 2007 | Nicolas Sarkozy becomes president. |
| 2008 | Legislation tightening entry rules for immigrants' relatives is passed. |
| 2009 | France, along with the rest of the world, enters an economic recession. |
| 2010 | Government says it will set up a commission to study the extent of burka-wearing in France after President Sarkozy said such garments "undermine the dignity of citizens." France begins to dismantle Roma camps and to deport their residents back to Romania and Bulgaria, as part of a package of new security measures. |
| 2011 | Face veil ban comes into force. |
| 2012 | François Hollande is elected president. |

# FURTHER READING/INTERNET RESOURCES

Kedward, H. R. *France and the French: A Modern History*. New York: Overlook, 2007.

Lotz, Nancy, and Carlene Phillips. *Marie Antoinette and the Decline of French Monarchy*. Greensboro, N.C.: Morgan Reynolds, 2004.

Popkin, Jeremy. *History of Modern France*. Upper Saddle River, N.J.: Prentice Hall, 2004.

Roberts, Lisa. *France*. Northborough, Mass.: Chelsea House, 2003.

Sypeck, Jeff. *Holy Roman Empire and Charlemagne in World History*. Berkeley Heights, N.J., Enslow, 2002.

## Travel Information

travel-guides.com/data/fra/fra.asp

www.franceway.com

## History and Geography

www.cia.gov/library/publications/the-world-factbook/geos/fr.html

## Culture and Festivals

www.franceway.com/culture/culture2.htm

www.lonelyplanet.com/destinations/europe/france/culture.htm

## Economic and Political Information

www.insee.fr/en/home/home_page.asp

www.nationmaster.com/encyclopedia/Politics-of-France

**advocates:** People who stand up on behalf of a cause or group of people.

**ally:** A person, group, or state joined in association with another.

**appeasement:** The political strategy of pacifying a potentially hostile nation in the hope of avoiding war.

**armistice:** A truce in a war to discuss peace terms.

**assimilate:** To integrate someone into a larger group so that differences are minimized or eliminated.

**bicameral:** Having two separate legislative houses.

**deported:** Forced to leave a country.

**dialect:** A regional variation of a language.

**discrimination:** Unfair and unequal treatment of people based on their race, culture, religion, sex, appearance, or some other quality.

**Druids:** Priests in an ancient religion practiced in Britain, Ireland, and Gaul until the people of those areas were converted to Christianity.

**economies:** The wealth and resources of countries.

**edict:** A formal proclamation.

**electoral college:** A body of electors who officially elect the president and vice president of the United States.

**extremist:** Someone who has extreme or fanatical beliefs and is willing to go to extremes by taking violent action to support those beliefs.

**genocide:** The systematic killing, or an attempt to do so, of all the people of a particular national, ethnic, or religious group.

**gross domestic product (GDP):** The total value of all goods and services produced within a country within a year, minus net income from investments in other countries.

**hate crimes:** Harassment, violence, or threats against people because of their race, religion, sexual orientation, or some other quality.

**humanist:** Someone committed to improving the lives of other people.

**hunter-gatherers:** Members of a society in which people live by hunting and gathering only, with no crops or livestock raised for food.

**hydroelectric:** Having to do with power that's generated by falling or flowing water.

**Jacobeans:** Supporters of King James I.

**literacy:** The ability to read and write on a functional level.

**nationalize:** To transfer a business or property from private to government control.

**nominally:** In name only, without power.

**precedent:** An action or decision that can be used as an example for future decisions.

**prejudice:** Having to do with something that exists in name more than practice.

**recession:** A period when businesses and finances produce less.

**renewable:** Capable of being replaced rather than being used up permanently.

**reparations:** Compensation demanded from a defeated nation by the victor in a war.

**resolution:** A legal decision.

**service sector:** The business segment that offers services rather than products.

**terrorism:** Taking action that's specifically intended to terrify people as a way to make people do what the group wants.

**tolerance:** The ability to accept people and ideas different from yourself.

**unicameral:** Having one legislative house.

# INDEX

## PICTURE CREDITS

# About the Authors and the Consultant

## Authors

Jeanine Sanna lives in upstate New York with a variety of animals. In addition to being an author and journalist, she is interested in the field of forensic chemistry. Jeanine also enjoys traveling, music, and theater.

Shaina Carmel Indovino is a writer and illustrator living in Nesconset, New York. She graduated from Binghamton University, where she received degrees in sociology and English. Shaina has enjoyed the opportunity to apply both of her fields of study to her writing and she hopes readers will benefit from taking a look at the countries of the world through more than one perspective.

## Series Consultant

Ambassador John Bruton served as Irish Prime Minister from 1994 until 1997. As prime minister, he helped turn Ireland's economy into one of the fastest-growing in the world. He was also involved in the Northern Ireland Peace Process, which led to the 1998 Good Friday Agreement. During his tenure as Ireland's prime minister, he also presided over the European Union presidency in 1996 and helped finalize the Stability and Growth Pact, which governs management of the euro. Before being named the European Commission Head of Delegation in the United States, he was a member of the convention that drafted the European Constitution, signed October 29, 2004.

The European Commission Delegation to the United States represents the interests of the European Union as a whole, much as ambassadors represent their countries' interests to the U.S. government. Matters coming under European Commission authority are negotiated between the commission and the U.S. administration.